THE POETRY OF LUTETIUM

The Poetry of Lutetium

Walter the Educator

Silent King Books

Copyright © 2024 by Walter the Educator

All rights reserved. No part of this book may be reproduced in any manner whatsoever without written permission except in the case of brief quotations embodied in critical articles and reviews.

First Printing, 2024

Disclaimer
This book is a literary work; poems are not about specific persons, locations, situations, and/or circumstances unless mentioned in a historical context. This book is for entertainment and informational purposes only. The author and publisher offer this information without warranties expressed or implied. No matter the grounds, neither the author nor the publisher will be accountable for any losses, injuries, or other damages caused by the reader's use of this book. The use of this book acknowledges an understanding and acceptance of this disclaimer.

dedicated to all the chemistry lovers,
like myself

LUTETIUM

Rare and sublime,

LUTETIUM

Lies Lutetium, in the periodic line.

LUTETIUM

Its story untold, its mysteries profound,

LUTETIUM

A metal majestic, in nature's bound.

LUTETIUM

From distant stars, where chaos reigns,

LUTETIUM

Lutetium emerges, where cosmic rains

LUTETIUM

Shower down elements, in fiery dance,

LUTETIUM

Forging the universe, in its vast expanse.

LUTETIUM

With atomic number seventy-one it stands,

LUTETIUM

A beacon of wonder, across distant lands.

LUTETIUM

Its nucleus dense, with protons arrayed,

LUTETIUM

Neutrons nestled, in the atomic shade.

LUTETIUM

In the depths of Earth, it's scarce to find,

LUTETIUM

Yet its presence profound, in the human mind.

LUTETIUM

For in laboratories, it finds its way,

LUTETIUM

To aid in research, where scientists play.

LUTETIUM

A luminescent gem, in crystal arrays,

LUTETIUM

Lutetium shines, in spectral displays.

LUTETIUM

Its glow mesmerizing, under ultraviolet light,

LUTETIUM

A testament to nature's artistic might.

LUTETIUM

From medical marvels, to industrial might,

LUTETIUM

Lutetium's utility, a guiding light.

LUTETIUM

In cancer's grasp, it finds its place,

LUTETIUM

Targeting tumors, with surgical grace.

LUTETIUM

In catalysts and lasers, it finds a role,

LUTETIUM

Advancing technology, towards a goal.

LUTETIUM

Its properties unique, its uses diverse,

LUTETIUM

Lutetium's legacy, it shall traverse.

LUTETIUM

Yet beyond its function, lies a deeper tale,

LUTETIUM

Of ancient cities, where echoes prevail.

LUTETIUM

Lutetia once stood, in the land of Gaul,

LUTETIUM

A testament to history's ceaseless call.

LUTETIUM

In the heart of Paris, its memory lingers,

LUTETIUM

A whisper of the past, where time's fingers

LUTETIUM

Trace the steps of ancients, in streets so fair,

LUTETIUM

Where Lutetium's name, finds its share.

LUTETIUM

So let us ponder, this element rare,

LUTETIUM

Its journey through time, beyond compare.

LUTETIUM

From the crucible of stars, to human hands,

LUTETIUM

Lutetium's story, forever stands.

LUTETIUM

ABOUT THE CREATOR

Walter the Educator is one of the pseudonyms for Walter Anderson. Formally educated in Chemistry, Business, and Education, he is an educator, an author, a diverse entrepreneur, and he is the son of a disabled war veteran. "Walter the Educator" shares his time between educating and creating. He holds interests and owns several creative projects that entertain, enlighten, enhance, and educate, hoping to inspire and motivate you.

Follow, find new works, and stay up to date
with Walter the Educator™
at WaltertheEducator.com

www.ingramcontent.com/pod-product-compliance
Lightning Source LLC
LaVergne TN
LVHW051921060526
838201LV00060B/4113